Eating Disorders

The Quest for Thinness

Edward T. Welch

New Growth Press
www.newgrowthpress.com

New Growth Press, Greensboro, NC 27404
Copyright © 2008 by Christian Counseling & Educational Foundation. All rights reserved. Published 2008

Cover Design: The DesignWorks Group, Nate Salciccioli and Jeff Miller, www.thedesignworksgroup.com

Typesetting: Robin Black, www.blackbirdcreative.biz

ISBN-10: 1-934885-49-5
ISBN-13: 978-1-934885-49-9

Library of Congress Cataloging-in-Publication Data

Welch, Edward T., 1953-
  Eating disorders : the quest for thinness / Edward T. Welch.
    p. cm.
  Includes bibliographical references and index.
  ISBN 978-1-934885-49-9
  1. Eating disorders—Patients—Religious life. 2. Eating disorders—Religious aspects—Christianity. I. Title.
  BV4910.35.W45 2008
  248.8′627—dc22

                                    2008011930
Printed in China
24 23 22 21 20 19 18 17   10 11 12 13 14

Do you ever wish that you could just forget about food? What started as an innocent diet has turned into a monster. You eat too little. You eat too much. You restrict. You binge. It's getting harder to cover up what you are doing. At first you tried exercise, then vomiting, then laxatives. Maybe you tried cutting too. Who would have thought that food—or the fear of it—would become the center of your life? Heroin, cocaine, and other street drugs lead to addictions. But food?

For you food is no longer . . . just food.

You know, of course, that you are not alone; many people struggle with eating disorders. It's easy to see why. Advertisers sell their products using only one slim body type; movies show impossibly thin, surgically enhanced heroes and heroines; high-profile athletes have body fat percentages that can only be maintained with round-the-clock workouts; food is everywhere; and more than half the U.S. is on a diet. In some countries food is nutrition. Here food is nutrition, but it also means beauty, control, comfort, guilt, shame, love, and loathing.

Food Problems Start Small

You began life with normal eating habits: You ate when you were hungry and didn't eat when you were full. But in a weight-conscious world, where food is used for comfort, you take small steps and "normal" gradually disappears. You want to be thin, so you become more serious about dieting. You like how food makes you feel, so you overeat and binge. Those who are close to you start noticing that food is becoming your obsession. You don't see it because your obsession has tricked you into thinking you are doing better than ever. But the truth is that your struggles with food have gained momentum, and you have become anorexic, bulimic, or both.

What Is Anorexia?

Anorexia is all about *not eating*. It is an all-consuming

fear of fat that leads you to starve yourself. Your fear might also lead you to try constant exercising, vomiting, and/or taking laxatives. What happens when these things don't make you feel any better? Your next step might be another form of self-punishment such as cutting. When others try to help you, it's easy for you to make them your enemy. You don't want *anyone* standing between you and what you believe you need.

What Is Bulimia?

Bulimia is all about *overeating*. A lot of food eaten secretly and rapidly is its trademark. In contrast to anorexia's control, bulimia is impulsive and out of control. Anorexia wants control, and seems to invite pain. Bulimia feels out of control, and wants comfort and relief. The two seem like complete opposites, but eventually, as your struggles with eating continue, they might look almost the same (see *Figure 1*). If you start as an anorexic, sooner or later you might use the same weight-loss strategies as someone with bulimia. If you are bulimic, you might also use the anorexic devices of self-punishment and food restriction to make up for a binge.

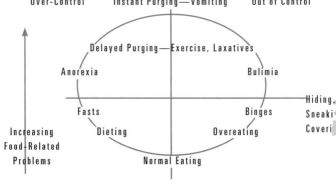

FIGURE 1: A MAP OF FOOD-RELATED PROBLEMS

How Did You Get Stuck?

How did you get into this cycle? Most people enter this cycle as a way of dealing with troubling, unwanted feelings—anger, pain, loneliness, guilt, self-loathing, and so on (see *Figure 2*). Without knowing what to do with your emotions, you starve them by restricting food or comfort them by binging on food. You might feel a little better temporarily, but at some point you have to eat again, or purge what you have eaten. So you break one of your many food laws. Then you feel horrible again. So you punish yourself by starving your feelings or soothing them with food, and the cycle continues. Like a hamster on a rotating wheel, you keep running, even though you aren't getting anywhere. You have a sense that there is no way out, but you distract yourself by binging, purging, or restricting. If you stop running, the hopelessness catches up to you, so you keep going, afraid to stop and afraid to think about the future. Without noticing how it happened, you've become a slave to your own food rules.

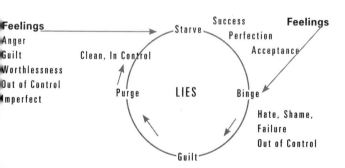

FIGURE 2: A TYPICAL ENSLAVING CYCLE FOR ANOREXIA AND BULIMIA

Breaking Free

If this comes close to describing your life, don't let hopelessness win. There is a way to break out of this cycle. It starts with you being open to the possibility that deep-down your problem is spiritual. Read the words of two people who struggle with eating problems:

> "Success through dieting was the key to my salvation. Success meant a perfect career, perfect control over my life—all of which depended on a perfect me—which depended on me living inside a perfect body."
>
> "Eating is one area of my life that no one can reach, not even God."

Doesn't it sound as if they're describing a religion? They have laws, rituals, sacrifice, penance, idols of comfort, idols of control, and the hope of salvation. The difference is that God is not in it. This is a lifestyle that tries to manage life apart from God. Take a moment to think about what your own food rules and rituals are. How are you using your "food rules" to manage your life?

Your problem isn't new. The apostle Paul, in the Book of Galatians, tells how we are always trying to construct our own religion. When Galatians was written, people were trying to use circumcision as a way to make themselves acceptable to God. Now we use different rituals, but it all comes down to the same thing: We believe we can be made right by something we do.

You might not be thinking about God at all, but deep inside you there is a desire to be "right" and "acceptable." It's easy to substitute yourself or other people as the final judge of what it means to be right. Instead of trusting in God, you trust in yourself and in your system of food laws to make you right.

If you are thinking about God at all, you probably believe that you have to become a better person before you can have a relationship with him. You're hoping that your own laws will show you the way. Meanwhile, you are constructing a world that has no room for God. Your food rules are actually keeping God away from you. The apostle Paul explains how this works in the Book of Galatians. At first glance, it might seem to you that Paul isn't talking about your struggle at all. But, as you read, replace "circumcision" and "the law" with your food rules and rituals, and you will see that he is talking about you and your struggle with food.

> It is for freedom that Christ has set us free. Stand firm, then, and do not let yourselves be burdened again by a yoke of slavery. Mark my words! I, Paul, tell you that if you let yourselves be circumcised [*follow food rules and rituals*], Christ will be of no value to you at all. Again I declare to every man who lets himself be circumcised [*follow food rules and rituals*] that he is obligated to obey the whole law [*every food rule perfectly, never any mistakes, never any failures*]. You

who are trying to be justified [*made right*] by law [*your own food rules*] have been alienated from Christ; you have fallen away from grace. But by faith we eagerly await through the Spirit the righteousness for which we hope. For in Christ Jesus neither circumcision nor uncircumcision [*neither eating too much, nor eating too little*] has any value. The only thing that counts is faith expressing itself through love. (Galatians 5:1–6)

There is a way out: "by faith," "through the Spirit," and "faith expressing itself through love." It is not rule keeping that saves you; it is your faith in Jesus that makes you clean, holy, and right (Romans 1:17; 8:1).

Sound easy? It is. It's rest rather than work. It's trust in another rather than independence. But, as you probably know, trust might be the last thing you want to do. Your quest for independence is one reason you dabbled in eating problems. You know that trust means giving up your own religion where food is at the center, and you are not likely to give that up easily. The only way you could trust God is to be absolutely certain that he is trustworthy. And he is.

How do you know that? Find out for yourself by looking at what God did when he came to earth as a man. Pick up a Bible, and read a little bit every day from the Gospel of John. Underline everything you read that shows you how trustworthy Jesus is. Notice especially how he treated people; think about why he died, and what his resurrection means for you. Jesus gave up his life for you. You can trust him with your life today. You can give up your food rules and follow him. You can "cast all your anxiety on him because he cares for you" (1 Peter 5:7).

Practical Strategies for Change

The number one reason people stay stuck in self-destructive patterns is that they don't really want to change. Of course, you don't like the consequences of your food obsession—the perforated esophagus, the rotting teeth, and the many other things that result from it, but there are parts of it you believe you can't live without. What if you gain weight and get fat? You have limits on how much you will trust God. You insist on having an out when you need it; you believe if you abandon your secret behaviors you will not have any resources to deal with life. You might want to get rid of the bad consequences of your obsession, but you don't want to give up the obsession.

Reluctance to Change Is Not a Deal-Breaker

Start by admitting how reluctant you are—this might be the first honest thing you have done with your obsession in a long time. And reading this article means you are willing to check out your options. So keep going.

Now listen to what you are saying. Every time you starve, every time you binge, you are saying something. What is it?

> "I need nothing."
>
> "I must be in control."
>
> "I am hurt. I want to feel nothing."
>
> "I am angry. I will show them."
>
> "I am bad. I will deny myself."
>
> "I am disgusting. I will be who I am and do something disgusting."
>
> "I am empty, alone. I want to feel full."
>
> "If only I could be nothing."

All these statements have one thing in common:

They are the feelings of someone living in a world where God is absent or very far away. You live in a kingdom that is not ruled by God. So you cry on your bed, but you don't cry out to the Lord (Hosea 7:14).

Cry Out to God, He Will Meet You

You don't turn to God for two reasons. One, you believe he will take away something you need—something you trust in. Two, you don't believe you are good enough to come to God. The truth is, all you have to do is turn to him and speak honestly, and he will meet you.

- God meets the hurt with compassion. "He heals the brokenhearted and binds up their wounds" (Psalm 147:3).
- God meets the angry and promises justice. "Do not take revenge, my friends, but leave room for God's wrath, for it is written: 'It is mine to avenge; I will repay,' says the Lord" (Romans 12:19).

• God meets the self-loathing by taking their shame on himself. "Therefore, there is now no condemnation for those who are in Christ Jesus." And, "as the Scripture says, 'Anyone who trusts in him will never be put to shame'" (Romans 8:1; 10:11).

Confess

You expected judgment and a deaf ear; you get the God who loves you and hears you. A relationship with him should be tempting. If you want a relationship with God, respond to him in the same way you respond to someone who loves you, someone you have been avoiding. Tell God that you have been wrong. Confess your sins.

Confess that your world is about you rather than him. Confess that you are living as if you know better than God. Confess that you are trying to save your own life rather than lose it (Matthew 10:39). Confess that you are trying to make life work apart from Jesus.

Get to Know God

You might expect that what comes next is a new system of rules, but God is different from our expectations. God's Word does show us how to live wisely and well in this world, but first you need to rest. "In repentance and rest is your salvation" (Isaiah 30:15). Don't do anything; just sit there!

Sit and learn who God really is. You are drowning under layers of wrong thinking about God. Start with the truth that Jesus is God. Everything you want to know about the true God can be found in him. So keep your eyes pealed for Jesus. Keep reading the Gospel of John. You can also read about Jesus in Matthew, Mark, and Luke. Keep in mind that Jesus is the King who got off his throne, humbled himself, came to earth, and died an awful, shameful death for you (Philippians 2:6–11). His death paid the penalty in full for your wrongdoing. You are tempted to think that you have to pay some of it yourself because no one has ever offered such forgiveness and love to you. But God is not like a person. He pays it all. You just say "thank you."

Whenever you think you have to pay him back for your uncleanness and sin, stop immediately. That might sound very religious, but it is your old religion talking. The true gospel is that you have been given an extravagant gift of forgiveness. It does sound too good to be true, but it is true.

Here are some ways to test whether you are still following your old religion or you are following Jesus:

- Do Jesus and his grace have the last word? Or are you still trying to keep your food laws?
- Have you ever held out your hands and shown Jesus that you have nothing to bring to him? All he asks of you is that you admit that you have nothing to bring and he has brought everything for you.
- Are you beginning to have joy?

Develop a Plan

There is still much to do, but if you put your trust in Jesus rather than yourself, then you have done the hardest part. Now you need to learn how to live wisely.

- *Ask for help.* This is another test of whether or not you really want to change. Are you willing to ask for help? Anorexia and bulimia are very private. If you are willing to talk with someone else, you are taking a big step in breaking the cycle. God's wise plan includes a community, and that should include wise mentors who follow Christ. You might also add physicians and dieticians.
- *Speak truthfully.* When you speak with others, be alert to your tendency to lie and cover up. The language of truth might not come easy for you, but you will find that you are blessed when you live in the light.

- *If you binge and purge, put structures in place to keep you from purging.* This will allow you to experience the consequences of your behavior. Purging is like a drug that removes consequences and the opportunity to grow in wisdom through them. Try eating in public and declaring the bathroom off-limits for at least an hour after meals.

- *If you restrict, gradually introduce once-forbidden but healthy foods.* Those who restrict typically panic with a weight gain of a couple pounds after the introduction of "illegal foods." Don't forget, if you find yourself wanting to run to your old ways, you are still trusting in your control rather than God's. Confession is the way to deal with your panic.

- *Be especially alert to how you respond to failures.* Sometimes you will purposely fail, fall into self-pity, believe that God has abandoned you, and revert to your old religion. Remember that when you fail (and you will; we all do), it's an opportunity to know that you rest in Jesus Christ rather than your own successes or failures. Then your failures will become times to be thankful that Jesus forgives you and never leaves you (John 14:18).

Your progress will be like that of everyone else who follows Jesus—bumpy with ups and downs. But don't forget: You are no longer isolated and on your own. You have the power of God by his Spirit, and the Spirit assures you that he will keep working in you until King Jesus returns (Philippians 1:6).